I AM SOMEONE ELSE
Poems About Pretending

Collected by Lee Bennett Hopkins

Illustrated by Chris Hsu

ini Charlesbridge

To Thomas Millins, principal, and the students at North Fort Myers Academy for the Arts in North Fort Myers, Florida, who truly know how to be someone else—L. B. H.

For Artemis, Mona, Niko, and Mallory—our next generation of imaginative thinkers—C. H.

Thanks are due to the following, all used by permission of the authors, who control all rights for their poem: J. Patrick Lewis for "Wild Child"; Amy Ludwig VanDerwater for "For a Little While"; Janet Clare Fagal for "A Mermaid's Tale"; Lois Lowry for "Big Problems"; Rebecca Kai Dotlich for "A Pirate's Life for Me"; Matt Forrest Esenwine for "The One"; Michelle Heidenrich Barnes for "Bellies, Bones, and Paws"; Heidi Bee Roemer for "A Suit of Blue"; Joan Bransfield Graham for "Nurse: Healing Hand"; Lawrence Schimel for "On a Clear Day"; Darren Sardelli for "Cool Creations"; Prince Redcloud for "One Day"; Lee Bennett Hopkins for "What a Poet Can Do"; Michele Krueger for "Dancing Child"; and Douglas Florian for "Video Game Hall of Fame." All © 2019.

At the time of publication, all URLs printed in this book were accurate and active. Charlesbridge, the author, and the illustrator are not responsible for the content or accessibility of any website.

Published by Charlesbridge
85 Main Street
Watertown, MA 02472
(617) 926-0329
www.charlesbridge.com

Library of Congress Cataloging-in-Publication Data
Names: Hopkins, Lee Bennett compiler. | Hsu, Chris illustrator.
Title: I am someone else: poems about pretending / collected by Lee Bennett
Hopkins; illustrated by Chris Hsu.
Description: Watertown, MA: Charlesbridge, 2018.
Identifiers: LCCN 2017055931| ISBN 9781580898324 (reinforced for library use)
  | ISBN 9781632897183 (ebook pdf) | ISBN 9781632897176 (e-book)
Subjects: LCSH: Imagination—Juvenile poetry. | Children's poetry, American.
Classification: LCC PS595.I46 .I25 2018 | DDC 811/.60809282—dc23 LC record
  available at https://lccn.loc.gov/2017055931

Printed in China
(hc) 10 9 8 7 6 5 4 3 2 1

Illustrations done in Photoshop
Display type set in Woodrow © 1997, 1999 Chank Diesel
Text type set in Horley OS MT © 1991 Adobe Systems Incorporated
Color separations by Colourscan Print Co Pte Ltd, Singapore
Printed by 1010 Printing International Limited in Huizhou, Guangdong, China
Production supervision by Brian G. Walker
Designed by Martha MacLeod Sikkema

Introduction

There is nothing better than being yourself. You are unique and special in every way. Once in a while it might be fun to think about becoming someone (or something!) else. Maybe someone imagined or someone you'd like to be when you grow up.

In this book fifteen poets write about who they might like to be, and they imagine themselves as a wizard, a firefighter, a video-game inventor, and more.

Who would you like to be? Just imagine!

—*Lee Bennett Hopkins, Cape Coral, Florida*

Wish!

Be a Storybook Character

Close your eyes.

Imagine what make-believe storybook character you might become (if you could).

Would you be . . .

a **wizard** double knotting moonbeams?

a **queen** wearing silken shoes and gown?

a **mermaid** exploring deep ocean caves?

a **giant's wife** stirring stew in vats and barrels?

a **pirate** swinging from ropes with telescopes?

Imagine!

Wild Child

J. Patrick Lewis

I am the elementary wizard
of P.S. 82.
You won't believe the wild-child,
wizardry things I do.

I pull scarves from evening
and wrap them around midnight.
I double knot six moonbeams
to dizzy the world with light.

If you get stuck in yesterday,
tell me; I'll set you free.
You cannot skip tomorrow
unless you skip with me.

Go ask my homeroom teacher:
she'll tell you who I am.
Now that we've met, she can't forget
this wizard—
   Alakazam!

For a Little While

Amy Ludwig VanDerwater

I close my door behind me.
At last I'm all alone.
My dress becomes
an ermine robe,
my chair a jeweled throne.
Dolls are my loyal subjects;
Teddy Bear is king.
My bedroom is a castle.
I wear a ruby ring.

I gaze into a looking glass.
I see my golden crown.
I whirl a waltz with Teddy
in my silken shoes and gown.

Tomorrow I will ride my mare
across this gentle land.
Peasants from the countryside
will come to kiss my hand.

But now I feel like playing ball.
I'll take a final twirl.
I'm done with being queen today.
It's time to be a girl.

A Mermaid's Tale

Janet Clare Fagal

I will be a mermaid,
dress in gauzy blue.
Splash around, flap my tail;
a wish I'll make come true!

I'll drift upon a foamy sea,
sleep on creamy sands.
Search everywhere for spiny shells,
cradle fish friends in my hands.

Some days I'll journey far away,
explore deep ocean caves.
I'll feast on seaweed, sip sweet sun,
then float through turquoise waves.

A mermaid's life is what I need!
I'll settle by the coast.
All day I'll dive and swim and swirl.
It's what I love the most.

Big Problems

Lois Lowry

I took on a perplexing life
when I became a giant's wife.

He has a monstrous appetite,
says my cooking's a delight.

But one encounters real perils
when stirring stew in vats and barrels!

And I am in a total quandary
each time I try to do the laundry.

His sweaters could encase three cars;
his undies are the size of Mars!

I have to climb upon a chair,
stretch my arms to smooth his hair.

It is a complicated struggle
to hug or kiss or simply snuggle.

He's very dear; I'm not complaining.
I only wish I'd had some training!

There ought to be some branch of science
that gives advice to wives of giants!

A Pirate's Life for Me

Rebecca Kai Dotlich

I swing from ropes
    with telescopes,
shoo away rats with my boot.
I'm best of the best, meanest of all;
I'll snare you and plunder your loot.

I carve rain with me sword
as I captain the sea,
tossing mates overboard. . . .
Grim and ruthless I be!

I cry *argh* to the ocean,
    wail *yarr* to the sky,
as I snag me a sash,
a small patch for me eye.

Ahoy ye, hornswoggled!
Steer far away, by golly.
You shall pity the day
    you encountered Mad Ollie.

Support!
Be a Person Who Helps

Think ahead.

Imagine what job you might want when you grow up. In many jobs you can help others.

Who would you like to become?

You could be . . .

a **firefighter** who fights flames.

a **veterinarian** who examines bellies, bones, and paws.

a **police officer** who acts bravely.

a **nurse** who offers an outstretched hand.

a **pilot** who flies through cloud-free skies.

Serve!

The One

Matt Forrest Esenwine

I want to be the one who fights flames,
taming smoke and heat with hook and hose.
I want to be the one who drives the truck,
sirens wailing wherever it goes.

I want to be the one who saves lives,
no matter who they are or where they're from.
I want to be the one who wears the suit,
so one day I can be just like my mom.

Bellies, Bones, and Paws

Michelle Heidenrich Barnes

I button up my lab coat,
scrub my hands with soap,
check the day's appointments,
and grab my stethoscope.

Some patients will be nervous,
legs quivering like leaves.
I'll give them treats and cuddles
to make them feel at ease.

I'll look at teeth, eyes, and ears,
listen to their hearts,
examine bellies, bones, and paws,
write details on their charts.

When the workday's over
and my lab coat's shedding fur,
I'll remember every thank-you—
every nuzzle, kiss, and purr.

A Suit of Blue

Heidi Bee Roemer

Mother says
I can be anything.
More than anything,
I want to wear a suit of blue,
a badge and boots,
and bravely serve my community.

My teacher says
sometimes police officers
make mistakes.
So I will do my best
to treat each person fairly,
with the respect they deserve.
More than anything,
I want to help make people's lives better
and neighborhoods safer.

When I close my eyes,
I can dream anything.
More than anything,
I dream one day
I will grow up—
big, strong, wise.
I *will* be a police officer.

A peace officer.

Nurse: Healing Hand

Joan Bransfield Graham

I will be
an outstretched
healing hand.

I will
understand
what it
feels like
to be a leaf
adrift on
a rapid river.

I will be
a giver
of calm,
a cool cloth
of care.

I will learn
what to do
to lead
you back to
the strength
that is
     you.

On a Clear Day

Lawrence Schimel

Who could spend a day like this
    locked away inside?

I will race to the top of the hill
    with my arms spread wide.

I'll sit on a rock—my stone cockpit.
    I can't stop grinning.
Excitement will flood through me
    as propellers start spinning.

Skies are cloud-free.
    It is perfect flying weather.
Come aboard with me.
    Let's fly together.

Invent!

Be a Person Who's a Maker

What ideas do you have?

It's wonderful to create and invent and bring new ideas to our world.

Will you create like . . .

a construction worker building massive structures?

a chef taking time to make everything right?

a poet weaving words?

a modern dancer galloping over a grassy savanna?

a video-game inventor designing the greatest game the world has ever seen?

Create!

Cool Creations

Darren Sardelli

Wearing a hard hat,
boots on my feet,
I'll smooth out each sidewalk,
pave every street!

Driving a dump truck,
bulldozer, too.
Laying down train tracks.
I'll love what I'll do.

Water parks,
shopping malls,
skyscrapers,
schools.

I'll build massive structures
with all types of tools.

I'll come up with riveting,
groundbreaking plans.
I'll help shape the world
with my heart, head, and hands.

One Day

Prince Redcloud

Seeing
how patiently,
how carefully,
my father

    grills, broils,
    roasts,
    fills pastries,
    bakes;

how he takes time
to make
everything special,
everything right,

I know
one day
I will
become
a chef.

A chef—

like
him.

What a Poet Can Do

Lee Bennett Hopkins

I will be a poet.

I will weave words
to make you sigh,
laugh,
cry.

Explore
similes,
metaphors,
syllables
galore,

to show
what a poem,
what a poet
can do.

To show you—

      YOU!

Dancing Child

Michele Krueger

Music makes my body move!

Piano notes let me tiptoe carefully
across a forest floor.

Cello strings
remind me to bend my knees low,
make my fingers flutter.

I become a golden sunset
hovering on the horizon
to rhythmic drumbeats.

I start
      spinning,
      jumping,
      leaping,
      running,
      over a grassy savanna.

I am a horse in the wild.
I am a dancing child.

Video Game Hall of Fame

Douglas Florian

I love to play my video games.
I even love their funny names:
like Pokémon or Hey You, Pikachu!,
Angry Birds, and Star Fox, too.
I play the older games like Pong,
StarCraft, and Donkey Kong.
The new releases are a thrill.
To play them well takes special skill.
But what I really wish to do
is make a game that's truly new.
Invent a game of great design,
with features that are solely mine—
with wild action, awesome sound,
and graphics that indeed astound.
The greatest game the world has seen,
on every single video screen.

Imagine!
Wish!
Support!
Invent!
Be Someone Else!